Lou Lou Mae's Badge of Courage

by Kinjatta Dobbins

illustrated by Lisa Tingle

To my children, Lauren and Aiden – you're fun to be with!
To my Ideal Soul, my helpmate – Te Amo!
To my friends and family, thank you for putting up with all my emails and text messages.
My editor, your support was, in many ways, therapeutic.
And to all the Lou Lou Mae's out there – this is for you! Your courage inspires me!
- K.D.

A note from the Illustrator – can you find my initials, hearts and a friendly, little inch-worm hidden on each page for you?
- L.T.

No one would ever know Lou Lou Mae couldn't see just as well as everyone else.

When Lou Lou Mae was three years old, her mother noticed Lou Lou Mae bumped into things and struggled with objects right in front of her.

Lou Lou Mae's mother took her to the doctor, who noticed Lou Lou Mae couldn't see the symbols on the chart when her right eye was covered. She was blind in one eye.

As Lou Lou Mae grew older, the doctor did more eye tests to determine if her eye might get better, but sadly, Lou Lou Mae still couldn't see out of her left eye.

Right before Lou Lou Mae started kindergarten, her doctor gave her an eye patch. It would help to strengthen her seeing eye so she could see objects and words more clearly.

Like other kids her age, Lou Lou Mae enjoyed things like playing kickball and riding her bike.

She loved helping her mother bake cupcakes and cookies.

But most of all, Lou Lou Mae loved reading! Her nose was always stuck in a book.

Lou Lou Mae did have one problem, though. She couldn't stand wearing her eye patch out in public! It was ugly and too big for her face.

Lou Lou Mae never wore her eye patch to school even though her doctor said it would help. By third grade, she felt she didn't need her eye patch, but her mother encouraged her to wear it.

Lou Lou Mae's parents were always reminding her to wear the eye patch.

"Lou Lou Mae, you know you should wear your eye patch," her mother gently reminded her.
"The doctor said it would help you see more clearly," her father added.
But no amount of coaxing was going to persuade Lou Lou Mae to wear that big black ugly thing on her face.

Lou Lou Mae considered wearing her patch. It would make her parents happy, and they only wanted what was best for her.

"Maybe it won't be so bad if I wear it around the house," Lou Lou Mae admitted.

Every night before going to bed, Lou Lou Mae would secretly put on her eye patch and stare at her reflection, trying to get used to having it on her face.

Like a fashion model, she struck several poses in the mirror, but no amount of posing made her want to wear it.

She still despised it, no matter how many times she tried it on.

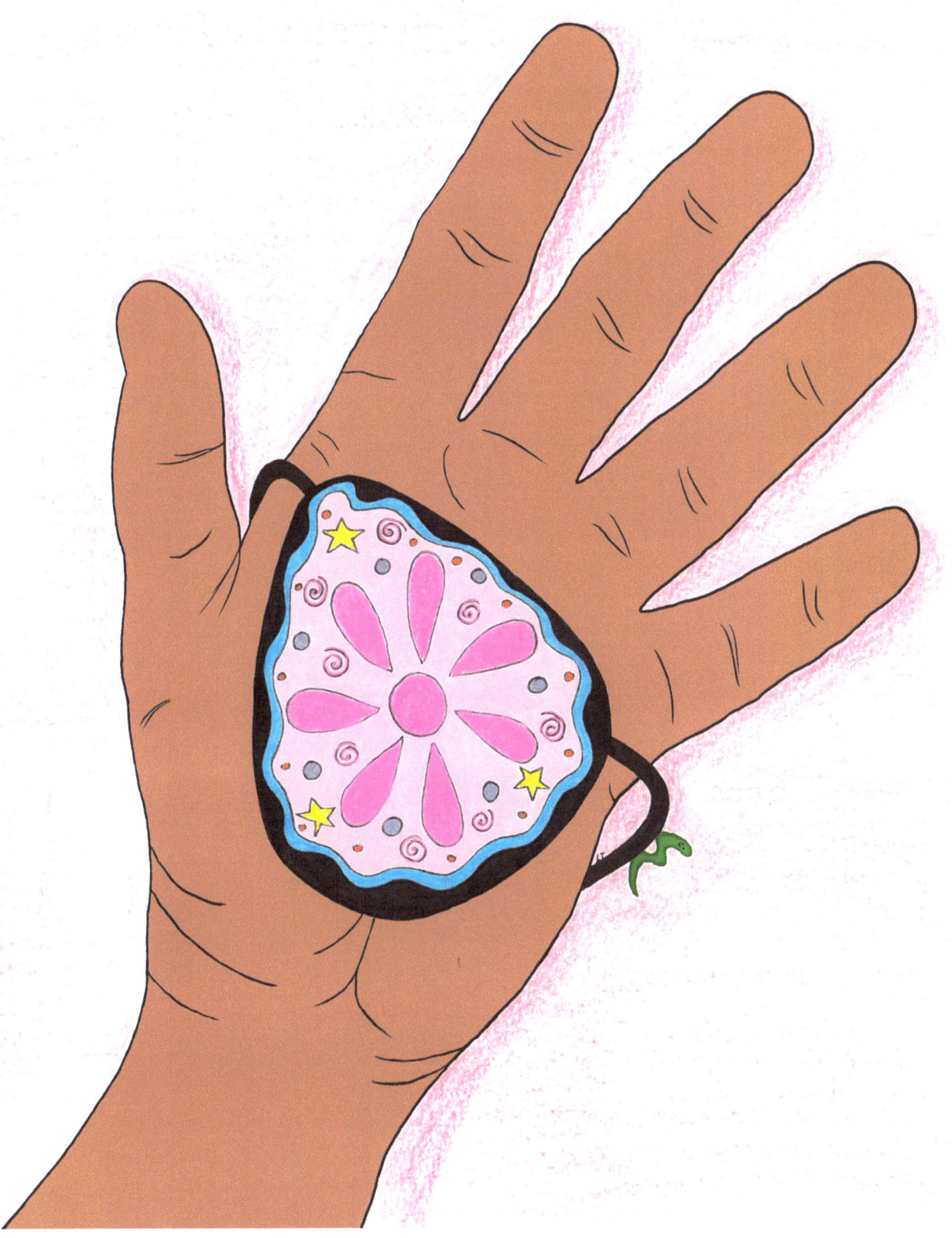

After decorating her patch, she put it on and looked in the mirror. Suprisingly, her reflection smiled back. She kind of liked the new patch.

But Lou Lou Mae still wasn't sure she could wear it out in public.

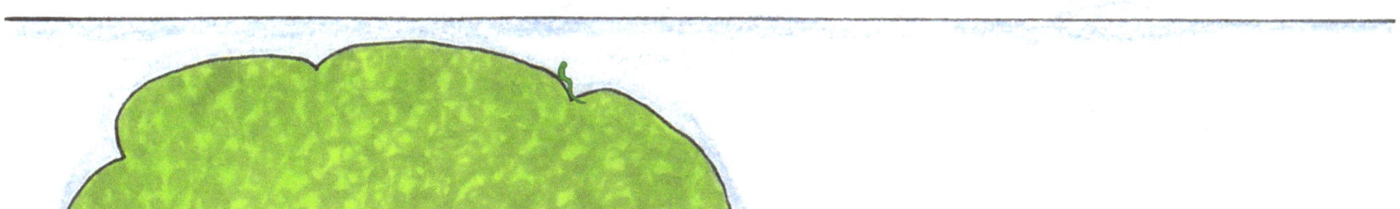

In the morning, Lou Lou Mae tucked the eye patch in the front pocket of her blue jeans for safe keeping.

Then she headed off to school, thinking lunchtime would be the perfect time to reveal her new look. Lou Lou Mae would show her parents she could wear her eye patch. "My family will be so proud!" she thought.

Sitting at her desk, waiting for twelve o'clock to strike, Lou Lou Mae tried hard to focus on her assignment. Finally, when the minute hand reached twelve o'clock, she blurted out, "Lunchtime!"

With her hand still pressed to her pocket, Lou Lou Mae got her lunch bag and lined up with the rest of her class.

Once her class reached their lunch table, Lou Lou Mae whispered to herself, "It's now or never." While no one was looking, she slipped her hand into her pocket and pulled out her patch. Butterflies banged and bumped against the walls of her stomach. Her heartbeat felt like drums being played on her chest. Lou Lou Mae wasn't ready to put on her eye patch, so she pushed it back into her pocket.

While Lou Lou Mae was eating her lunch and giggling with friends, the bell rang. She forgot about putting on her patch. "Maybe another day, another time," thought Lou Lou Mae.

Lunchtime was over. The kids scurried to dump their trash into the garbage bin then lined up to head back to class.

The children shuffled into their classroom, put away their lunch bags, and sat quietly on the rug to wait for story time.

"Today, class, we have a special visitor," Lou Lou Mae's teacher announced. "Instead of story time, Mrs. Valor is going to speak to us about courage. She's a veteran, a person who has served in the United States military."

"Good afternoon, students! I am Staff Sergeant Valor, but you can call me Mrs. Valor. I recently retired from the United States Army. I was responsible for many soldiers, just like your teacher is responsible for you. I helped my soldiers reach their full potential. I am honored to be here to speak to you today about courage."

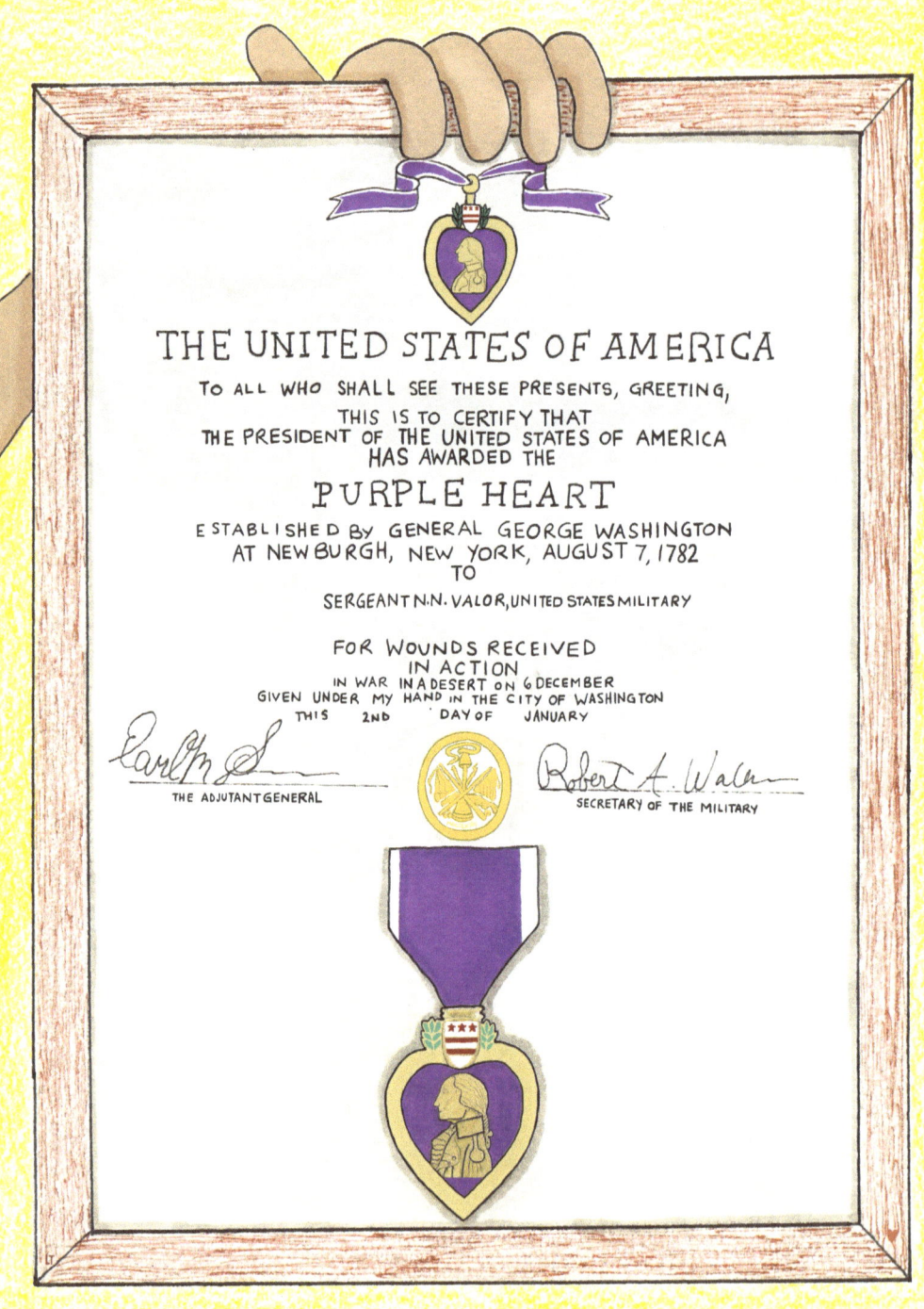

Mrs. Valor had everyone's attention. Guest speakers were rare, and she looked like she had something important to share. "I was injured while helping save the lives of members from my company." "Wow!" chimed the class.

The students began to edge a little closer to Mrs. Valor, who was sitting in the teacher's rocking chair.

"As you can see, part of my right leg is missing. Now I wear a prosthetic, an artificial limb." Mrs. Valor tapped her leg. "After my leg was injured, doctors were able to save part of my leg, and once I healed, my doctor fitted me for this cool prosthetic, which allows me to do many things you can do."

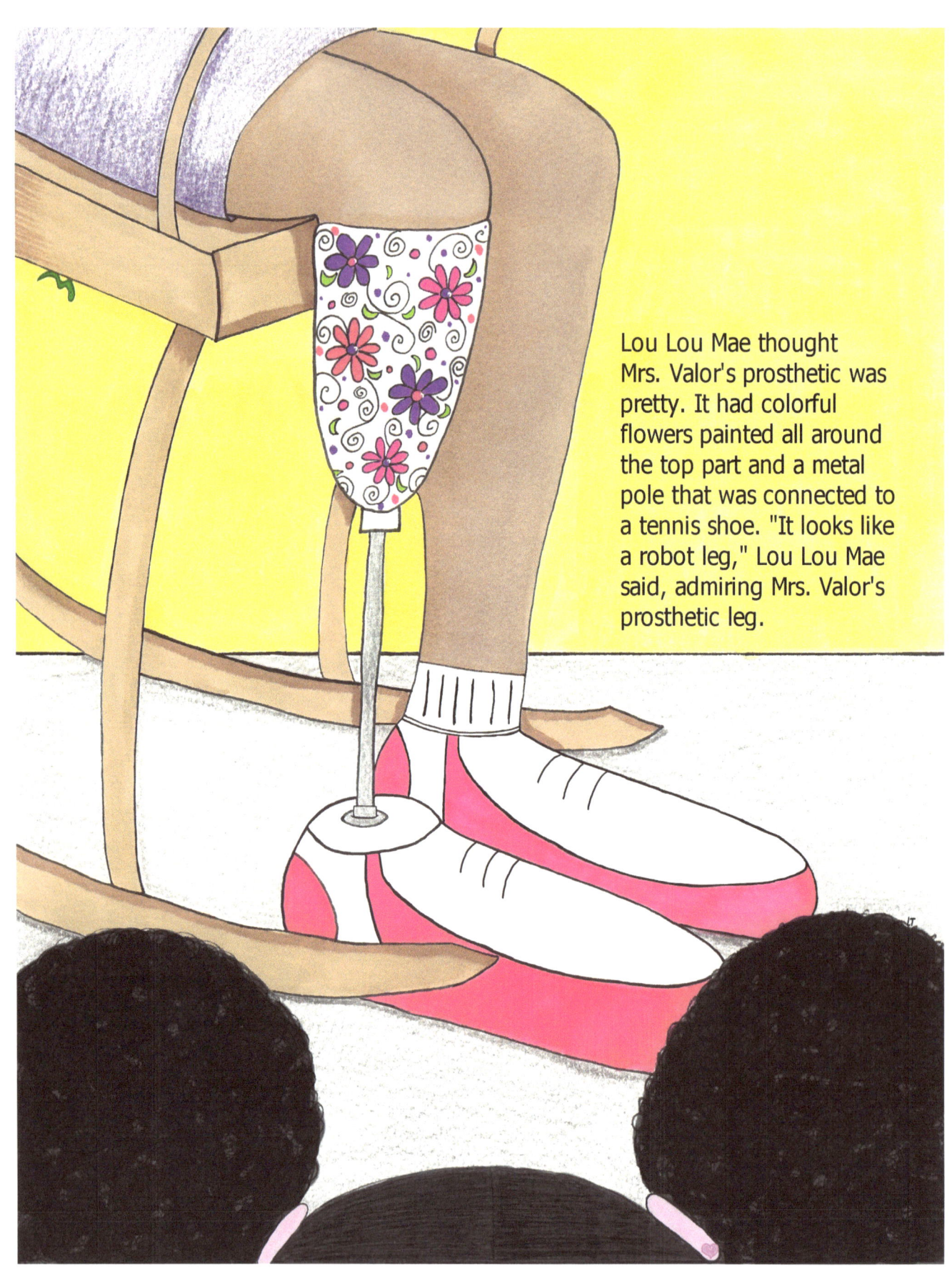

Lou Lou Mae thought Mrs. Valor's prosthetic was pretty. It had colorful flowers painted all around the top part and a metal pole that was connected to a tennis shoe. "It looks like a robot leg," Lou Lou Mae said, admiring Mrs. Valor's prosthetic leg.

Mrs. Valor got up from the chair and walked slowly around the students sitting quietly on the rug. "See, children, I can jump, skip, and even hop on one leg. I can do just about anything any two-legged person can do." Mrs. Valor demonstrated several cool moves for the children.

All around Lou Lou Mae, her classmates gasped as Mrs. Valor performed hip-hop moves all the third graders knew.

"Students, I want to be honest with you – when doctors told me I would lose part of my leg because it was severely injured, I was afraid. I didn't know what my life would be like with a prosthetic. Would I be able to drive a car the same way I did before the injury? Would I walk funny?..."

"...I like to run in marathons, but would I be quick enough to make it to the finish line? And the thought of people staring or pointing at me made me want to hide from everyone."

Lou Lou Mae felt sorry for Mrs. Valor, but she did not seem sad at all. She looked happy! "How can someone be happy with part of a leg missing?" Lou Lou Mae wondered.

Lou Lou Mae had always thought of herself as courageous, but lately, she hadn't been feeling very brave. She touched the eye patch in her pocket. "If Mrs. Valor can boldly wear her prosthetic, then I can wear my patch," Lou Lou Mae assured herself.

Mrs. Valor motioned for the students to follow her to the back of the classroom, where she taught the children a special march and her favorite motto. With legs marching up and down, Mrs. Valor belted out, "There's nothing to it but to do it. There's nothing to it but to do it."

Even Lou Lou Mae's teacher joined in on the fun as everyone marched around the classroom, singing, "There's nothing to it but to do it. There's nothing to it but to do it."

The end of the day was quickly approaching, and Mrs. Valor had to say her goodbyes — but not before one last, "There's nothing to it but to do it. There's nothing to it but to do it."

That's when Lou Lou Mae raised her hand as high as the sky. She wanted to make sure the teacher saw her.
"Yes, Lou Lou Mae. Do you have a question?"

Lou Lou Mae stood up and took a deep breath. "Yes, I have something to share." She reached into her pocket, pulled out her patch, and showed it to Mrs. Valor.

"My doctor gave me this patch before I started kindergarten. I'm blind in my left eye. And when I wear my eye patch, I can see better out of the other eye," Lou Lou Mae admitted. "Until today, I wouldn't wear my patch in public. I was afraid people would stare and make fun of me." Tears began to fall down Lou Lou Mae's cheek. "But your story helped me see that being brave isn't the same as not being afraid. It's moving forward and believing you'll come out a winner!"

Then, to everyone's surprise, Lou Lou Mae put on her patch. After a few adjustments to make sure it was on correctly, Lou Lou Mae smiled. "There's nothing to it but to do it!"

"I am proud of you! I understand the courage it took for you to put your patch on in front of your classmates," Mrs. Valor said.
Lou Lou Mae's classmates gathered around her and gave her high fives and pats on the back.
"Hip, hip hooray for Lou Lou Mae!" chanted the class.

Beaming, Lou Lou Mae puffed out her chest, pushed back her shoulders, and held her head up high. She understood that courage didn't mean never being scared. It meant facing the difficult times with bravery and knowing things would be okay in the end.

"There's nothing to it but to do it!"

Kinjatta Dobbins was inspired to write *Lou Lou Mae's Badge of Courage* after an encounter with a stranger who helped her overcome her fear of wearing her own eye patch in public. Seeing this stranger wear a beautiful turquoise eye patch was the inspiration she needed to wear her patch and to write this story. Kinjatta lives in San Antonio, with her husband and children.

Lisa Tingle's fun and sometimes silly illustrations appeal to all ages. A proud member of SCBWI, she is a passionate artist who loves to make an author's words come to life. Lisa graduated with a BS from Texas A&M University, College Station, and is proud to be an Aggie! Lisa Tingle has always loved drawing, doodling, and getting lost in her art. Lisa and her husband, Jeff, have three children and live in San Antonio, Texas. Her other illustrations can be found at The Twig Bookstore, on Facebook, on Instagram and at https://www.scbwi.org/members-public/lisa-tingle.

www.ingramcontent.com/pod-product-compliance
Lightning Source LLC
LaVergne TN
LVHW072113070426
835510LV00002B/39